T

Teaching with *A Writer's Reference*

EIGHTH EDITION

Nancy Sommers, Harvard University

Welcome to the eighth edition of *A Writer's Reference*, now more useful and relevant than ever. The new edition is much more than a grammar reference or a citation guide. It's a real classroom tool with topics and models you'll find useful as you teach—thesis statements, evidence, analysis, synthesis, public speaking, and more. You may also notice an exciting change in how the handbook works. The eighth edition is an integrated tool that combines instruction in print with interactivity and practice in an online setting. LaunchPad allows you to use the handbook more actively as a classroom tool and allows your students to use the handbook more actively as a learning tool.

This tabbed section will help you make the most of the book as a classroom tool and will guide you in orienting your students to the print book and its e-Pages. You'll find practical suggestions for using the handbook to support your goals and assignments, save time, and engage students. You'll find specific ideas, strategies, and models for integrating and using the handbook as you teach your composition courses or any writing-intensive course. And you'll also learn about the different versions of *A Writer's Reference* that are available to you and your students.

Bedford/St. Martin's

Boston ◆ New York

Supporting your goals and assignments with *A Writer's Reference*

When students routinely use their handbook in the course, they see its value, find it's a faster avenue to answers than Google or other Web search engines, are more likely to rely on it as a reference, and are more likely to achieve the goals of the course.

Many writing instructors find it helpful to review the goals of the course during the first or second class period. When you discuss goals (your school may use the word *outcomes* or *competencies*), talk with students about how the course materials you've assigned will reinforce those goals.

When you discuss this course goal . . .	**You can point out this resource in the book or media . . .**
Students will use critical thinking and reading skills to analyze topics and source texts.	Writing guide for an analytical essay on pages 82–83
Students will ethically integrate the words and ideas of others (direct quotations, summaries, and paraphrases) into their own writing.	Exercises on integrating sources in the e-Pages
Students will reflect on their own development as writers.	Advice about reflective writing and portfolio keeping in C4

Other tips for reinforcing the goals of the course and specific assignments include the following:

- In your syllabus, inform students that the handbook's content will be useful in class and important for their success. Align specific sections of the handbook with specific course goals.
- Assign a scavenger hunt to help students familiarize themselves with LaunchPad. Ask them to find print pages or e-Pages that support concepts you emphasize in your course (peer review, MLA style, or revising, for example).
- When you give assignments, build in cross-references to the handbook that give students a jump start in learning and fulfilling the expectations of the assignment.

SUMMARY AND ANALYSIS ASSIGNMENT FOR ENGLISH COMPOSITION I, WITH REFERENCES TO *A WRITER'S REFERENCE*

Choose one of the following selections and write a three-to-five-page essay in which you summarize the work and respond critically:

Mike Rose, "I Just Wanna Be Average"
Emily Bazelon, "The Next Kind of Integration"
Garret Keizer, "Why We Hate Teachers"
Matt Miller, "First, Kill All the School Boards: A Modest Proposal to Fix the Schools"

A summary requires close, careful reading. A good summary (A1-c) explains the essential points of the essay to someone who hasn't read it.

A critical response (A1-d) presents your judgment of a piece of writing with a thesis (C1-c) and specific examples from the text. An effective response often raises a question about the author's position or examines the author's reasoning and logic (A3-a, A3-b).

Be sure to include an establishing sentence in your opening paragraph. In it, give the title of the reading and the author's name and present the author's rhetorical purpose/main idea. In your thesis, be sure to communicate your main idea about the text or your primary judgment of the text.

Shape paragraphs (C5-a, C5-b) so that their relation to your main point is clear. Integrate (MLA-3a, 3b) at least three specific passages from the text into your essay. Include a title, format your paper in MLA style, and include a works cited page (MLA-5b).

Notes for summary:	Due Tuesday, 2/17
First draft:	Due Thursday, 2/19
Peer review (C-3a):	Tuesday, 2/24
Final draft:	Due Tuesday, 3/3

NOTE: Even if you are assigning the handbook in a non-humanities course, building cross-references into your assignments can help set expectations and can save you time in the long run.

EXCERPT FROM A LAB ASSIGNMENT FOR BIOLOGY, WITH REFERENCES TO *A WRITER'S REFERENCE*

You already have the information you need for this assignment — it is in the notes you took while doing the experiment today. Now arrange this information in the correct format for a lab report. Be sure to include each of the following sections.

Abstract: This short paragraph summarizes your whole report. (See p. 125.) One way to think about writing the abstract is to have one or two sentences that capture the main ideas of each of the following sections.

Introduction: This section gives the background for your work. All the information necessary to understand your work (the experimental organism, the design, the aspect you have chosen to research) is presented here. Include your hypothesis in this section. A good rule of thumb in writing an introduction is to write it for a general audience (pp. 3 and 15) so that anyone, even your parent or grandparent, could understand why you did what you did.

Methods: Describe what you did and how you did it. Write this in the past tense (G2-f). Identify the control group for your study in this section.

Results: Put all of your experimental results in this section. If you can make a graph, chart, or table (C2-b) of your results, you should put it in this section. But don't just put it here — be sure to write about it and describe it.

Discussion: This section describes what *you* think about your results. Discuss your ideas about your results and why they worked the way they worked — or why they did not work the way you thought they would.

Your grade will be based on content and clarity (edit with sections S, G, and P). Be sure that the main point (C2-a) of the lab is clear in the report. Include all five sections, and be sure to place and label figures (C2-b) appropriately.

Designing writing assignments that integrate the handbook

Start with purpose and audience.

- Make the purpose of the writing assignment clear and connected to the learning objectives for the unit or the course. (C1-a)
- The intended audience should be explicitly stated: Is the audience a group of experts? Nonexperts? Other students? Potential clients? Those who might provide funding? If students are to choose the audience, say so. (C1-a)

Share specific criteria.

- What do you want students to be able to demonstrate with this assignment? (p. 7)
- Should students document sources in a particular style? (MLA, APA, CMS)

Direct students to models; emphasize format.

- Spend class time (fifteen minutes) walking through the features of a model paper—content features, format features, and rhetorical features. (See model papers in A1-e, A4-h, MLA-5b, APA-5b, and CMS-5b.)
- Determine whether you'll emphasize academic formats (essay, review, lab report) or professional formats (memo, market analysis, operator's manual) or a combination of the two in your course. (C6)

Use prompts that emphasize positioning and problem solving.

- Ask students to identify a debate and position themselves within that debate. A sample prompt could be "Our course readings have presented many angles on [topic x]. Write an essay in which you take a position on [x] and support it with evidence." (C1-c)
- Pose problems to help students improve critical/academic thinking. A sample prompt could be "Apply what you know about Smith's 'invisible hand' theory [concept x] to economic recovery in Haiti or another post-trauma economy [situation y]. How might the theory play out in practice?"
- In a writing-intensive technical course, a prompt such as the following would work: "Review the design specifications for [x]. Suggest one key change you would make to the design. Argue for your modification: What problem does it solve?" (A4)

Designing writing assignments that integrate the handbook, *continued*

Chunk out the tasks; provide interim deadlines.

- Divide the writing assignment into several steps or tasks, each with due dates. Scaffolding helps students avoid procrastination and plagiarism—and in general produces better writing.
- Provide opportunities for peer review. (See *Teaching with Hacker Handbooks*, a free supplement for instructors.)
- Build in time for revising. (C3)

Expect edited papers, but don't be the editor.

- Make time for peer editing sessions before the final paper or project is due.
- Encourage students to go to the writing center.
- If you point out surface errors in drafts, do so with codes from the handbook.

Include a rubric for grading.

- How can a student earn full points? Be specific about what percentage of the final grade depends on content features, format, and clear communication.
- Share samples of strong, average, and weak papers.

T2 Choosing the right version of *A Writer's Reference* to meet your needs

A Writer's Reference is published in several different versions to accommodate varying instructor needs, student needs, and course and program goals. All versions include the core book, the Classic version. All versions other than the Classic include additional content, most often in a separate tabbed section. In the version with exercises, the exercises are integrated throughout the book.

All versions are supported by the same instructor resources. See the catalog page at macmillanhighered.com/writersref/catalog. To examine any version, contact your sales representative.

A Writer's Reference (Classic)

Twelve tabbed sections offer class-tested help with composing and revising, academic writing, research and documentation (MLA, APA, and CMS [*Chicago*] styles), grammar and style, and document design—all in a tabbed, comb-bound, quick-reference format. 624 pages.

A Writer's Reference with Exercises

This version is tailor-made to use with your students in class or for additional out-of-class grammar practice—with plenty of items for multilingual students. It includes ninety-eight exercise sets integrated throughout so that the practice for each topic follows the explanations and examples. A helpful mix of exercise formats includes both sentence-length items and paragraph-length items. 688 pages.

A Writer's Reference with Writing in the Disciplines

To help your students write in composition and in other college courses, this version includes an additional tabbed section with advice and model papers in nine academic disciplines: biology, business, criminology, education, engineering, history, music, nursing, and psychology. The Classic version includes a section on writing in the disciplines, A6, and the writing in the disciplines version contains additional material that is an extension of that chapter. Model papers represent multiple genres: lab report, memo, proposal, reflective essay, concert review, technical report, researched essay, clinical practice paper, and review of the literature. 768 pages.

A Writer's Reference with Writing about Literature

If you ask your students to write analytically about works of fiction, poetry, and drama, this version will meet your needs. It gives advice on forming and supporting an interpretation, with an emphasis on avoiding plot summary; guidance for integrating literary quotations in MLA style; and advice on using secondary sources. The literature tab includes two annotated student essays, one of which is based on secondary sources. 688 pages.

A Writer's Reference with Resources for Multilingual Writers and ESL

This version offers multilingual writers targeted advice and strategies for college writing and research. It includes additional exercises, study skills help, advice about meeting college expectations, and sample academic writing by a multilingual student. 688 pages.

A Writer's Reference, Eighth Edition

A Canadian Writer's Reference

With examples that reflect Canadian culture and concerns and with spelling, style, and measurement changes for cultural relevance, *A Canadian Writer's Reference* is a practical, easy-to-use reference for students who are writing in courses taught at Canadian colleges and universities. This version also includes comprehensive coverage of writing about literature. 688 pages.

Additional content for custom handbooks

Understanding and Composing Multimodal Projects

If you ask students to compose multimodal projects, this content will provide students with the step-by-step instruction they need to successfully present or publish their work. Students learn how to understand and analyze multimodal texts such as advertisements, video essays, or slide presentations before composing their own. Detailed instruction provides guidance for students as they plan, draft, revise, and publish their projects. 112 pages.

Strategies for Online Learners

An ever-growing number of students are enrolled in online sections of first-year writing courses. This content addresses online students' needs by offering study tips and time management strategies. Topics include how to be an active participant in the course, how to navigate the learning space, how to communicate appropriately with peers and instructors, and how to seek academic help and other resources. 48 pages.

T3 Saving time with *A Writer's Reference*

A Writer's Reference is designed to be flexible—to be used both as a reference and as a tool for classroom and online instruction. As a reference text, it helps writers by giving advice and models when class is not in session or when an instructor is not available. *A Writer's Reference* offers straightforward advice for starting and planning an essay, crafting a thesis statement, gathering support, editing for style or correctness, finding and citing sources, designing a document, and much more.

A Writer's Reference can also save college writers time. It does so by offering quick access to reliable writing, reading, and speaking advice 24/7, which means that students don't have to hunt around randomly on the Web. Keep in mind that the book and its resources are designed to save you time as well—by giving you a shorthand system for marking surface errors and some specific activities that are ready-made for the classroom.

If a handbook is to serve as a classroom text, it must be easy to use, offer quick avenues to clear content, and support class activities and course goals. *A Writer's Reference* is such a text; it includes a variety of reference aids, and it supports writers and teachers with accessible advice, examples, and models.

T3-a Familiarize students with the handbook's reference aids.

Working from the outside in, you will notice several reference aids.

The main menu

The menu on the inside front cover gives you an overview of the book's contents, roughly organized in three sections: writing well, writing correctly, and writing with sources. Color-coded arrows point the way to the appropriate tabbed section. Common questions to the left of the arrows anticipate the help student writers may need.

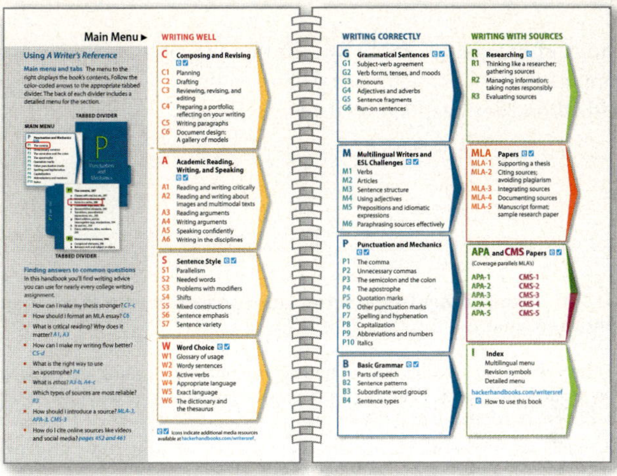

Main Menu ►

Using *A Writer's Reference*

Main menu and tabs The menu to the right displays the book's contents. Follow the color-coded arrows to the appropriate tabbed divider. The back of each divider includes a detailed menu for the section.

MAIN MENU / TABBED DIVIDER / TABBED DIVIDER

Finding answers to common questions In this handbook you'll find writing advice you can use for nearly every college writing assignment.

- How can I make my thesis stronger? C1-c
- How should I format an MLA essay? C6
- What is critical reading? Why does it matter? A1, A3
- How can I make my writing flow better? C5-d
- What is the right way to use an apostrophe? P4
- What is *ethos*? A3-b, A4-c
- Which types of sources are most reliable? R3
- How should I introduce a source? MLA-3, APA-3, CMS-3
- How do I cite online sources like videos and social media? pages 452 and 461

WRITING WELL

C Composing and Revising
- C1 Planning
- C2 Drafting
- C3 Reviewing, revising, and editing
- C4 Preparing a portfolio; reflecting on your writing
- C5 Writing paragraphs
- C6 Document design: A gallery of models

A Academic Reading, Writing, and Speaking
- A1 Reading and writing critically
- A2 Reading and writing about images and multimodal texts
- A3 Reading arguments
- A4 Writing arguments
- A5 Speaking confidently
- A6 Writing in the disciplines

S Sentence Style
- S1 Parallelism
- S2 Needed words
- S3 Problems with modifiers
- S4 Shifts
- S5 Mixed constructions
- S6 Sentence emphasis
- S7 Sentence variety

W Word Choice
- W1 Glossary of usage
- W2 Wordy sentences
- W3 Active verbs
- W4 Appropriate language
- W5 Exact language
- W6 The dictionary and the thesaurus

Icons indicate additional media resources available at hackerhandbooks.com/writersref.

WRITING CORRECTLY

G Grammatical Sentences
- G1 Subject-verb agreement
- G2 Verb forms, tenses, and moods
- G3 Pronouns
- G4 Adjectives and adverbs
- G5 Sentence fragments
- G6 Run-on sentences

M Multilingual Writers and ESL Challenges
- M1 Verbs
- M2 Articles
- M3 Sentence structure
- M4 Using adjectives
- M5 Prepositions and idiomatic expressions
- M6 Paraphrasing sources effectively

P Punctuation and Mechanics
- P1 The comma
- P2 Unnecessary commas
- P3 The semicolon and the colon
- P4 The apostrophe
- P5 Quotation marks
- P6 Other punctuation marks
- P7 Spelling and hyphenation
- P8 Capitalization
- P9 Abbreviations and numbers
- P10 Italics

B Basic Grammar
- B1 Parts of speech
- B2 Sentence patterns
- B3 Subordinate word groups
- B4 Sentence types

WRITING WITH SOURCES

R Researching
- R1 Thinking like a researcher; gathering sources
- R2 Managing information; taking notes responsibly
- R3 Evaluating sources

MLA Papers
- MLA-1 Supporting a thesis
- MLA-2 Citing sources; avoiding plagiarism
- MLA-3 Integrating sources
- MLA-4 Documenting sources
- MLA-5 Manuscript format; sample research paper

APA and CMS Papers
(Coverage parallels MLA's)
- APA-1 CMS-1
- APA-2 CMS-2
- APA-3 CMS-3
- APA-4 CMS-4
- APA-5 CMS-5

I Index
- Multilingual menu
- Revision symbols
- Detailed menu

hackerhandbooks.com/writersref
How to use this book

Tabs

The Classic version of the handbook has twelve tabbed dividers, or *tabs*; other versions may have thirteen. The front of each tab includes the code letter for that tabbed section. These code letters are used in index entries to help students flip quickly to the right section. The reverse side of each tab includes a list of contents for that tabbed section. The page range for the section is printed on the tab extension—the part of the tab that sticks out of the book.

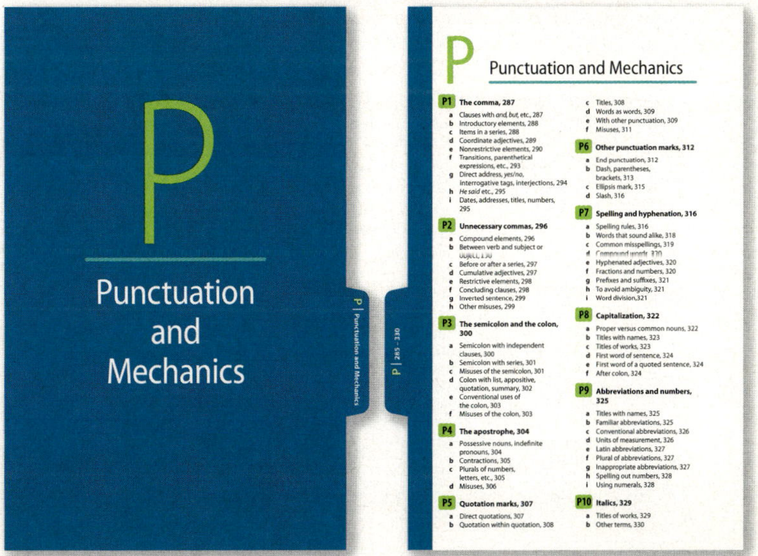

P Punctuation and Mechanics

P1 The comma, 287
- a Clauses with *and, but*, etc., 287
- b Introductory elements, 288
- c Items in a series, 288
- d Coordinate adjectives, 289
- e Nonrestrictive elements, 290
- f Transitions, parenthetical expressions, etc., 293
- g Direct address, *yes/no*, interrogative tags, interjections, 294
- h *He said* etc., 295
- i Dates, addresses, titles, numbers, 295

P2 Unnecessary commas, 296
- a Compound elements, 296
- b Between verb and subject or object, [illegible]
- c Before or after a series, 297
- d Cumulative adjectives, 297
- e Restrictive elements, 298
- f Concluding clauses, 298
- g Inverted sentence, 299
- h Other misuses, 299

P3 The semicolon and the colon, 300
- a Semicolon with independent clauses, 300
- b Semicolon with series, 301
- c Misuses of the semicolon, 301
- d Colon with list, appositive, quotation, summary, 302
- e Conventional uses of the colon, 303
- f Misuses of the colon, 303

P4 The apostrophe, 304
- a Possessive nouns, indefinite pronouns, 304
- b Contractions, 305
- c Plurals of numbers, letters, etc., 305
- d Misuses, 306

P5 Quotation marks, 307
- a Direct quotations, 307
- b Quotation within quotation, 308
- c Titles, 308
- d Words as words, 309
- e With other punctuation, 309
- f Misuses, 311

P6 Other punctuation marks, 312
- a End punctuation, 312
- b Dash, parentheses, brackets, 313
- c Ellipsis mark, 315
- d Slash, 316

P7 Spelling and hyphenation, 316
- a Spelling rules, 316
- b Words that sound alike, 318
- c Common misspellings, 319
- d Compound words, 320
- e Hyphenated adjectives, 320
- f Fractions and numbers, 320
- g Prefixes and suffixes, 321
- h To avoid ambiguity, 321
- i Word division,321

P8 Capitalization, 322
- a Proper versus common nouns, 322
- b Titles with names, 323
- c Titles of works, 323
- d First word of sentence, 324
- e First word of a quoted sentence, 324
- f After colon, 324

P9 Abbreviations and numbers, 325
- a Titles with names, 325
- b Familiar abbreviations, 325
- c Conventional abbreviations, 326
- d Units of measurement, 326
- e Latin abbreviations, 327
- f Plural of abbreviations, 327
- g Inappropriate abbreviations, 327
- h Spelling out numbers, 328
- i Using numerals, 328

P10 Italics, 329
- a Titles of works, 329
- b Other terms, 330

Codes

At the tops of the pages, you'll find the handbook's section codes (G5-c, for example). Some instructors find these helpful as a search device and as an aid when they respond to students' drafts.

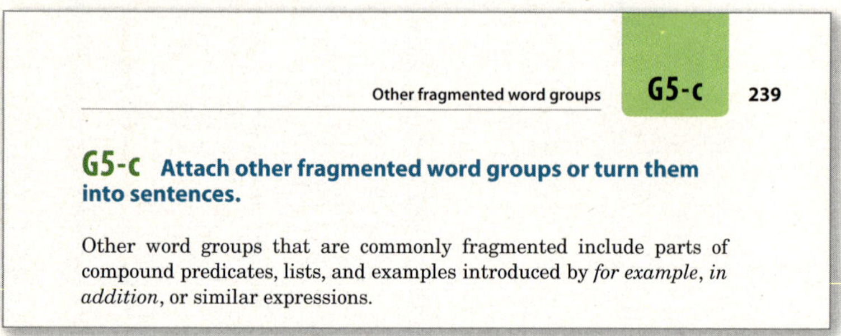
Other fragmented word groups G5-c 239

G5-c Attach other fragmented word groups or turn them into sentences.

Other word groups that are commonly fragmented include parts of compound predicates, lists, and examples introduced by *for example*, *in addition*, or similar expressions.

Boxes, charts, and checklists

These quick-reference devices serve as hubs of information. For many years, both teachers and students have told us how much they've come to rely on the many boxes, charts, and checklists in *A Writer's Reference*—pages that are often dog-eared by users because they offer at-a-glance summaries of key content.

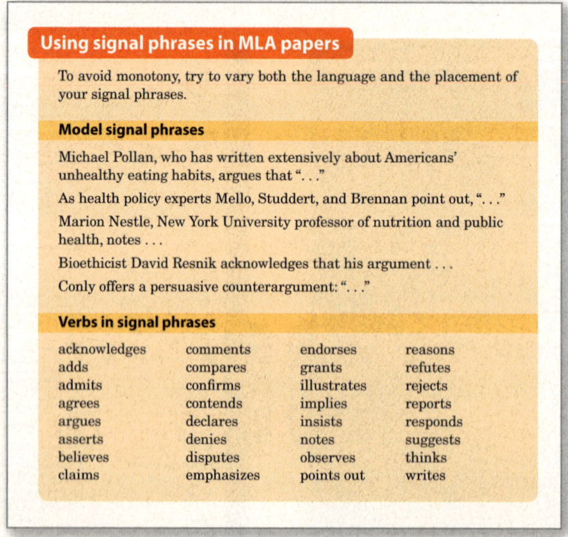
Using signal phrases in MLA papers

To avoid monotony, try to vary both the language and the placement of your signal phrases.

Model signal phrases

Michael Pollan, who has written extensively about Americans' unhealthy eating habits, argues that ". . ."

As health policy experts Mello, Studdert, and Brennan point out, ". . ."

Marion Nestle, New York University professor of nutrition and public health, notes . . .

Bioethicist David Resnik acknowledges that his argument . . .

Conly offers a persuasive counterargument: ". . ."

Verbs in signal phrases

acknowledges	comments	endorses	reasons
adds	compares	grants	refutes
admits	confirms	illustrates	rejects
agrees	contends	implies	reports
argues	declares	insists	responds
asserts	denies	notes	suggests
believes	disputes	observes	thinks
claims	emphasizes	points out	writes

Documentation directories

In each of the three style sections—MLA, APA, and CMS (*Chicago*)—students will find a directory of documentation models. Scanning the directory, organized by type of source, allows students to quickly find the model they need to cite their source.

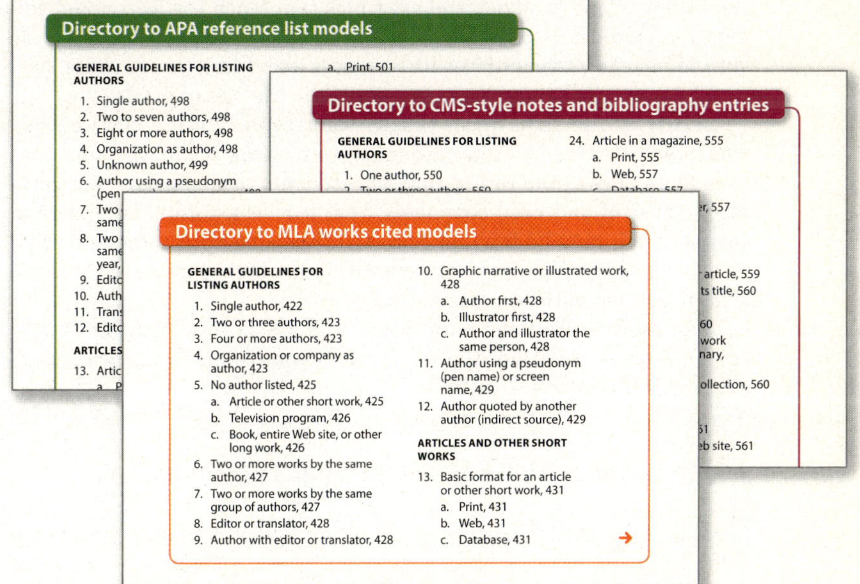

The index

The index, written to be user-friendly, includes traditional handbook terms alongside entries inspired by students' search practices and their own terminology. The index includes *dots* as well as *ellipsis mark*, for example, and *flow* as well as *coherence*. See tabbed section I.

Other reference aids

Turn to the back of *A Writer's Reference* and you'll see a detailed menu, or list of contents, that may come in handy as you respond to drafts. (Some teachers use codes to respond to surface errors: P1-b for commas with introductory elements or S4-a for shifts in point of view, for example.) Coming into the book from the back, you'll notice other useful reference aids: a menu that directs multilingual writers to targeted content and a list of revision symbols (*dev* and *sv agr*, for example) that may save you time when you write marginal comments.

T3-b Expect edited papers, but don't be the editor.

Using some of your comments to direct students to content in the handbook has the dual benefit of saving you time and teaching students how to find revision help in the handbook. You don't have to edit a student's subject-verb agreement errors; writing *G1* or *sv agr* in the margin will send the student to advice and examples that teach the lesson and will give you more time to comment at length on a more global concern. Be sure to have a conversation with students about how to use codes such as *G1* and *sv agr* before or as you return the first set of drafts.

Early in the semester, you may want to facilitate a class discussion about comments. You can share your ideas about the role that comments play in the course and ask students to share how they have made sense of and used comments from teachers, tutors, and peers in the past. You may be familiar with the "Revising with comments" feature in *A Writer's Reference* (section C3-a), which may help you have that discussion with your students.

For more on responding to your students as they plan, draft, and revise, request a copy of the free professional resource *Responding to Student Writers.* (See p. IE-28.)

T3-c Facilitate skill building through LearningCurve.

If you find you need to cover grammar, style, and punctuation topics with the whole class or a few students, the online components of LaunchPad for *A Writer's Reference* will help. Students can build and practice skills on their own time, and you can easily keep track of their progress. The LearningCurve exercises (available for twenty-nine common topics) are adaptive, which means that the program personalizes the practice for students, offering more or less difficult items in response to a student's progress through the exercise. Easy reporting gives you a view of success by student or by class.

hackerhandbooks.com/writersref
- e G5 Sentence fragments > Exercises: G5–3 to G5–7
- ✓ G5 Sentence fragments > LearningCurve: Sentence fragments

References in the print book direct students to exercises in LaunchPad's e-Pages for practice.

T3-d Assign and give credit for editing logs.

When you ask your students to keep track of their learning by charting the errors they make and the corrections they try, you are encouraging a long-term writerly habit *and* saving yourself time. Students can create editing log pages where they record the following:

1. an incorrect sentence from their own writing
2. the handbook section number and rule that helps them revise the sentence
3. the corrected sentence

For a sample, see page 31. As a final assignment, you can ask students to reflect on what they learned from keeping an editing log.

T4 Engaging students with *A Writer's Reference*

Once students understand that a particular resource is going to help them become stronger, more successful learners, they pay attention; they engage. You can help them realize the usefulness of their handbook, its power to help them collaborate with others, and the *<ahem!>* fun of adaptive learning.

T4-a Introduce the handbook.

Begin by introducing the handbook to let students know how you plan to use it in class and how you expect students to use it outside of class. You may want to use this as a moment to reflect on what a reference is and how it differs from other kinds of textbooks or resources for writing that students might find on the Web.

To orient your students to the book's major reference aids—the menus, the index, the documentation directories, and so forth—you can assign the tutorials that are located in LaunchPad (hackerhandbooks .com/writersref). Some instructors design scavenger hunts so that students can locate key coverage in the book—coverage that matches the course goals—*before* they need it. See hackerhandbooks.com/teaching for sample scavenger hunts.

What follows are several activities, all collaborative, that teachers can use at the beginning of the semester to introduce the handbook.

- ***The revision memo.*** Have students read and review a draft written by a former student (you will need a piece of writing from a previous semester). Assign students to discuss the following questions in a peer group: What are the draft's strengths and problems? What specific revision strategies will improve the draft's readability, and why? Where in the handbook might the student go for advice? Ask students to write a brief memo in which they recommend three or four revision goals and use the handbook's coding and language to explain, for instance, how to develop a stronger thesis statement, unify paragraphs, or revise run-on sentences.
- ***The scavenger hunt.*** Pair students to complete a scavenger hunt to locate key coverage in the handbook—coverage that matches the course goals and assignments. The search actively encourages students to navigate the handbook's index, menus, charts, and

checklists—hubs of information—and to find specific help before they need it.

- ***Understanding expectations.*** When you give students their first assignment, or a rubric for the first assignment, have them work together to annotate it with cross-references to the pages and sections of the handbook they will need to successfully complete the assignment. Ask students to answer these questions: What do you need to know how to do in order to complete this assignment? Where in the handbook will you find guidance? This exercise also helps students learn to carefully read assignments and rubrics so that they understand expectations.
- ***Leading the class.*** To reinforce the idea that the handbook contains useful vocabulary for talking about writing, ask each student to teach a handbook lesson to a group of peers. Allow students to choose their lesson—how to analyze a Web source or how to replace passive verbs with active ones, for example—and use the handbook's language and examples for the lesson.

Here's an excerpt from a scavenger hunt for a course that focuses on writing argument papers.

EXCERPT FROM A SCAVENGER HUNT

8. Section _____ gives advice about writing thesis statements. I found a sample of a well-written thesis statement on page _____.
9. Guidelines for active reading can be found on page _____.
10. Samples of annotated readings (readings with student notes on them) are in this section: _____.
11. Section _____ gives advice about using specific evidence in argument papers.
12. Section _____ covers how to evaluate another writer's argument. Pages _____ give advice on judging how a writer represents different viewpoints.
13. I found the sample argument essay on page _____.
14. There is a sample MLA-style works cited page on page _____.

T4-b Ask students to bring the handbook to class; use it in class.

A Writer's Reference is handy and portable. If you're using an e-book version of the book, it's even more so. Require that students have it in class with them. Here are three easy ways to engage students in an activity that teaches a rhetorical concept and draws on the handbook:

- ***Try the "So what?" test (p. 11).*** Pair students and ask them to take turns sharing a draft of an opening paragraph that includes a thesis statement. Have them discuss each other's draft by answering the "So what?" question. Have each writer make notes about how to revise.
- ***Try analyzing a sample paper (pp. 42–43).*** In preparation for assigning reflective writing, ask students to read the "Key features" of a reflective letter and then, in pairs or small groups, to identify those features in the sample reflective writing by Lucy Bonilla.
- ***Try the double-entry notebook experiment (p. 74).*** As a class, examine the sample notebook entries. Discuss the differences between the content in the left column and that in the right column. For a reading you have assigned, give students twenty minutes to start making entries in their own double-entry notebook.

T4-c Make the most of examples and models.

A Writer's Reference is full of examples and models, ready to be consulted in class. Students benefit from seeing examples of

- the kinds of sentences they are trying to craft or correct
- tasks they are attempting for the first time (such as annotating a reading or constructing an outline)
- the bibliographic entries and in-text citations they need to use when working with sources
- the kinds of papers they are expected to compose
- large writing projects divided into manageable tasks

During a whole-class activity, students can turn to relevant pages in the print book—or you can project the pages from the e-book version of *A Writer's Reference* on your laptop.

Many instructors take class time to review one or more of the book's examples as part of a lesson. On page IE-19 is one teacher's lesson plan on drafting debatable thesis statements.

For additional lesson plans that make the most of the handbook's examples, see *Teaching with Hacker Handbooks*, available as a free download (hackerhandbooks.com/teaching) or as a free print resource from your sales representative.

SAMPLE IN-CLASS ACTIVITY

Drafting debatable thesis statements

The purpose of the activity is to help you understand what *debatability* means, why it is essential for an effective thesis statement, and how you can turn a factual thesis statement into a debatable one.

Whole class:

1. Review C1-c in *A Writer's Reference*. Consider the concept of *debatability*.
2. What makes a point debatable? As a class, we'll make a list of points that are debatable, as well as a companion list of facts. (Debatable point: Hybrid vehicles are the single most important technological development in the last twenty-five years. Fact: Hybrid vehicle sales continue to rise worldwide.)

Small groups:

3. Review the example of the thesis statement that is too factual, the one about the polygraph, on page 11. What is the *problem* with the draft thesis? What *strategy* is suggested for revising it? What additional strategies can you come up with?
4. Discuss the revised thesis. How does it differ from the draft thesis? What is the debate on this topic? What is an example of a counterpoint that an opponent could make after reading this thesis?

Whole class:

5. As a class, rough out an outline for a paper that uses the revised thesis statement.

Homework: Take a fact from the list we created in step 2 above. Use the handbook's suggested strategies — identifying a debate and posing a question — to rewrite this fact as a thesis statement. Put your thesis to the "So what?" test. Due Thursday, January 29.

T4-d Use e-Pages activities in LaunchPad to engage students in their own writing.

Students in a writing course should be doing writing instead of just reading about writing. The e-Pages within LaunchPad offer students prompts and a space in which to write—a place to practice applying the lessons of the handbook to their own drafts. "As you write" prompts in the e-Pages make the handbook's content meaningful and useful.

As you write: Planning with sources

Read three sources that you are considering for your research project. Ask yourself how each source will function in your project. Consult section R3 to understand the various ways to use sources to develop your points. In the space below, write brief notes about what role each source will play in your paper. Will it offer background information, an explanation of a key term, an alternative interpretation, expert testimony, or something else?

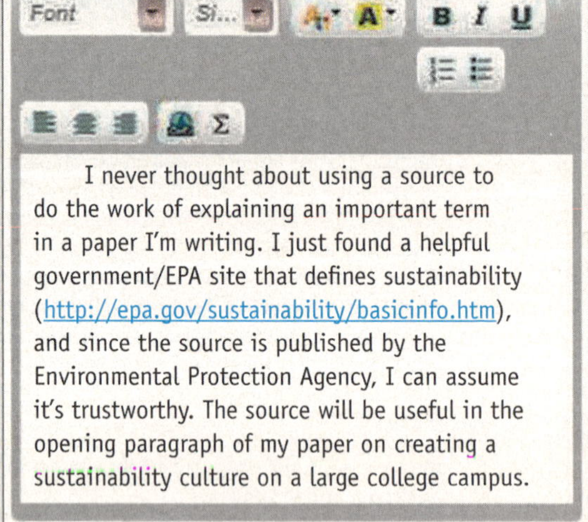

Writing prompts in the e-Pages help students apply handbook lessons to their own writing.

T4-e View video tutorials in class or assign them for homework.

We have included a series of video tutorials in LaunchPad to help students familiarize themselves with the topics in the handbook, the reference aids, and the ways in which the handbook will help them in their writing course and in any other college course that requires writing. In short, the tutorials help them see the *value* in using and owning their handbook.

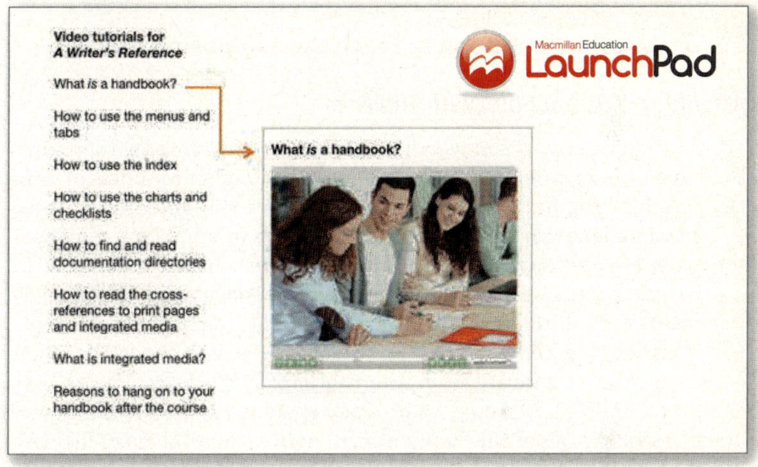

T5 Integrating *A Writer's Reference* into your course: Classroom activities

This section offers a sampling of specific teaching ideas and classroom activities that ask students to draw on the handbook for support. For more detailed suggestions and customizable teaching materials, visit hackerhandbooks.com/teaching or contact your sales representative for a copy of *Teaching with Hacker Handbooks*.

T5-a Use the handbook to teach the composing process.

Activity 1: Experimenting with audience

When students have a solid draft of an essay, a report, or another paper that they are writing, ask them to imagine an audience different from the one they originally intended. Ask them to write an entirely different introduction with this alternative audience in mind (you may have them review *audience* in C1-a). You might even have students write a brief reflective statement or discussion post about how the changes they made for a different audience would change the paper in general.

A variation of the activity: Ask students to look at one of the model papers on the companion Web site (hackerhandbooks.com/writersref) or in the handbook (A1-e or A4-h). They should (1) imagine a different audience for the paper they've chosen, (2) write a journal entry identifying the specific alternative audience, and (3) describe how the claims would need to change in order to satisfy audience expectations.

Activity 2: Revising with comments

Before you return the first set of drafts, it's helpful to spend time as a class discussing some of the comments you typically write to students on drafts. Show samples of comments you have written on student papers in the past. Engage students in a discussion about how they might revise based on your comments.

Extension: Give a set of drafts back to students. Have them work in pairs to use the advice and strategies in the "Revising with comments" section (C3-a) to determine a revision plan for at least one area of each of their drafts.

In the e-Pages: Ask students to complete one or both of these activities in LaunchPad: As you write: Using reviewers' comments or As you write: Being a peer reviewer.

T5-b Use the handbook to teach thesis statements and the parts of an essay.

Activity 1: Preparing to draft thesis statements

As a class, brainstorm a few issues that are topics of hot debate at your school right now. Has the school implemented new academic requirements? Has anyone offered a proposal for new student parking or housing? Is your school about to adopt a service learning/volunteering requirement for all students? Choose three to five topics and break the class into as many groups as you have topics. At this point, no one is taking a side on any issue. Each group should talk for five minutes about what types of evidence could be used as support: News articles? Interviews? Statistics? After each group presents possible evidence to the class, ask students to select one topic to be the focus of the thesis statement they will draft.

Review section C1-c as a class; talk about the thesis as an answer to a question, a resolution of a problem, or a position within a debate. As a class, write a few thesis statements and then break into small groups again. Ask the groups to apply the questions in the "Putting your working thesis to the 'So what?' test" chart on page 11 as they evaluate the draft thesis statements.

For an alternative classroom activity, see M1, "Teaching thesis statements," in *Teaching with Hacker Handbooks*, a free supplement for instructors.

T5-c Use the handbook to teach argument and analysis.

Activity 1: Identifying claims and counterarguments

Ask students to work collaboratively, in pairs or small groups, to analyze either the sample analytical essay on pages 80–81 or the sample argument essay on pages 107–11. As preparation for a writing assignment of their own, ask them to read through the model paper and identify the central claim, the supporting claims, and the counterargument. Depending on the context or lesson, you could also ask them to identify the types of appeals the writer uses, the purpose and audience for the paper, or what makes the thesis debatable.

In the e-Pages: Ask students to complete one or both of these activities in LaunchPad: **As you write: Drafting your central claim and supporting claims** or **As you write: Practicing counterargument**.

Activity 2: Practicing critical reading

Practice critical reading and annotating as a class. First, read the examples of annotated texts on pages 72–73 and 86. Ask students to (1) discuss how annotating a text might help a reader understand the text, (2) add to the writer's annotations by making one of their own, and (3) share their annotation with a partner. Then have students read a new text, a brief two- or three-paragraph article. Encourage students to mark up the text, circling key terms, asking questions in the margin, and challenging the author's assumptions. Finally, combine the students' annotations to create a set of critical notes on the work. A docucam or projector can be helpful for this activity.

In the e-Pages: Ask students to complete one or both of these activities in LaunchPad: As you write: Reading actively or As you write: Developing an analysis.

Activity 3: Preparing to write a summary

X-raying (outlining) a text is good practice for writing a summary. Just as an x-ray allows a viewer to see a skeleton, x-raying a piece of writing is an exercise in identifying the structure of a text. Have students practice x-raying a reading by using different color highlighters (if they are working with a photocopy). Ask them to identify the writer's thesis, or claim, in one color and the main lines of the writer's argument—in other words, the supporting evidence—in another color. See the sample on page 76, an outline of the brief article on pages 72–73.

T5-d Use the handbook to teach the research process.

Activity 1: Starting research with a question

Using section R1-b, talk as a class about how research begins with asking a question. Ask students to practice posing possible research questions that might help them begin the research process. As a class, brainstorm examples of questions that are too broad, too factual, or too speculative (see R1-b for examples), and then ask students to test the questions (see p. 11) and present revisions of those questions. You might also want to use R1-b as a springboard to talk about the differences between a topic and a question.

In the e-Pages: Ask students to complete this activity in LaunchPad: As you write: Pose questions worth exploring.

Activity 2: Preparing to write an annotated bibliography

Take a look at the sample annotated bibliography in the handbook's e-Pages and at the sample entry on page 387 in the handbook. Discuss the annotated bibliography writing guide with students to help them understand the expectations and features of the genre. Either as a distinct assignment or as a step in a researched essay assignment, ask students to select a few sources and write annotations for the sources in a working bibliography, following the guidelines in the Writing Guide and the example in the handbook. Ask students to bring to class one entry from their annotated bibliography. Discuss the questions that an annotation should answer: What is this source's main point? How does this source relate to your thesis? How does this source relate to other sources you are using? Why is this source worth using for your project?

In the e-Pages: Ask students to complete this activity in LaunchPad: As you write: Developing an annotated bibliography.

Activity 3: Using signal phrases

Academic writers and journalists depend on signal phrases (MLA-3b, APA-3b, CMS-3b) to integrate the words and ideas of others into their own writing. Distribute one or two pieces of writing that rely heavily on sources. Ask students to mark up the texts, identifying any signal phrases (*Benson suggests that . . .* ; *The director of Homeland Security argues that . . .*). Talk about the different roles that signal phrases play: as boundary markers, as glue, to identify an expert, to introduce counterpoints, and so forth.

T5-e Use the handbook to teach grammar, style, and punctuation.

Activity 1: Determining the severity of surface errors

In any discipline, errors that impede meaning (such as sentence fragments) halt communication more than does the occasional missing apostrophe. To help your students think critically about degrees of error, have them work collaboratively to create an Err-O-Meter that measures the seriousness of different kinds of errors for their intended audience. You might also discuss why certain errors are more serious for some audiences than for others.

Extension: Have students create a class guide to the most serious errors, including tips for checking for the errors and a list of the sections of the handbook that address fixing the errors. (Adapted from a *Bits* post by Barclay Barrios at Florida Atlantic University. Visit macmillanhighered.com/bits for more teaching ideas.)

T5-f Use the handbook to teach visual literacy.

Activity 1: Reading a visual text critically

Ask each of your students to bring an advertisement to class—either a print ad or a printout of an online ad. As a class, look over the sample annotated ad on page 86. Pay particular attention to the annotations. What is the student writer asking and noticing? Ask your students to contribute additional annotations. What do they notice or wonder about as they look at the Equal Exchange ad?

As students annotate their own advertisement, point them to page 86 for an example. During the next class period, ask students to do a bit more writing about their ad, responding to the questions in the "Guidelines for analyzing an image or a multimodal text" chart on page 88. Their responses can become notes for a first draft of an analytical paper.

In the e-Pages: Ask students to complete one or both of these activities in LaunchPad: As you write: Reading visual texts actively or As you write: Analyzing an image or a multimodal text.

Activity 2: Determining the purpose of visuals in professional writing

Bring four or five examples of professional writing to class; be sure each document includes at least one visual. It's best if the pieces are fairly brief (one to five pages). You might choose a report, a newsletter, a memo, one section of a scholarly article, a popular article, a brochure, or part of a user's manual. The visuals could be diagrams, photographs, tables, charts, or maps. Break your class into as many groups as you have documents. Each group should review the chart on pages 18–19, "Choosing visuals to suit your purpose." Have each group spend twenty to thirty minutes (1) identifying each type of visual used in the document, (2) identifying the purpose of the document, and (3) discussing whether the type of visual is best suited to the author's purpose and how the visual is or is not helping the author communicate an idea. Each group can share its findings with the whole class.

T6 More support for instructors

More ways to integrate *A Writer's Reference* into your course

Teaching with Hacker Handbooks, a collection of resources designed to accompany all four Hacker handbooks, is a full instructor's manual that will help you integrate a handbook into your composition or writing-intensive course. Part I includes chapters that address broad teaching topics. Part II offers ten teaching modules, each including a discussion of common writing challenges, a single assignment or class activity, and a directory to additional resources. Part III includes handouts, assignments, sample syllabi, and rubrics drawn from composition instructors around the country. A complete list of the contents follows.

Teaching with Hacker Handbooks

Part I Topics

Part II Modules

Part III Sample Course Materials

Available in print or online

Teaching with Hacker Handbooks

Marcy Carbajal Van Horn, formerly of St. Edward's University
Jonathan S. Cullick, Northern Kentucky University
Sara McCurry, Shasta College
272 pages
ISBN: 978-1-4576-61829-1

Professional resources

You can also request free professional resources such as the following at macmillanhighered.com/teachingcentral.

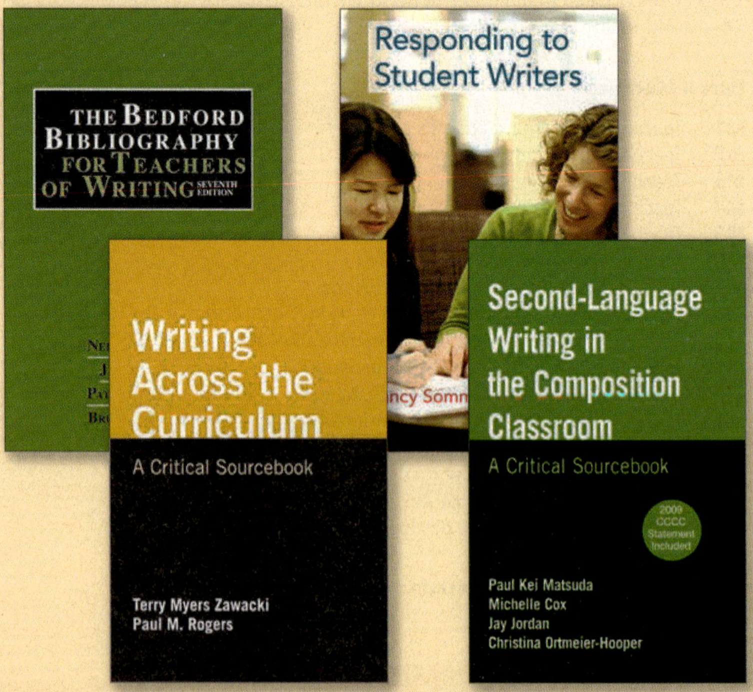

Tips for responding to student writers

Reading drafts and providing feedback to student writers about their ideas are the most difficult and time-consuming parts of any teacher's job. It is important work, however, and a critical contribution to a writer's development. The following tips for providing feedback to your students are adapted from *Responding to Student Writers* (Nancy Sommers), a free professional resource published by Bedford/St. Martin's.

Tips for responding to student writers

Preparing to respond

- ***Be positive.*** The goal of commenting is to offer encouragement and honest assessment. Look for strengths and help students build on strengths.
- ***Take turns.*** Think of responding as teaching, not correcting—especially in early drafts. Responding is most fruitful when you engage students in a dialogue—a conversation between writer and reader.
- ***Share models.*** Share with students a rough draft and final draft of the same paper; let them see that true revising is often an architectural renovation project—not just patchwork and fixes.
- ***Discuss the purpose of comments.*** Spend class time talking with students about the purpose of comments. Introduce them to the types of comments you give and explain any symbols or shorthand you use. Talk with students not only about how they can use comments to help them revise a specific piece of writing, but also about how they can apply those comments to future writing assignments.

Responding to rough drafts

- ***Go global.*** Resist asking students to patch and edit before they develop their ideas. Asking students to think about grammar, punctuation, and word choice in sentences that may not make it to the next draft could be a waste of both your time and theirs. Turn students' attention to larger, more global issues of organization and focus.
- ***Know when to go local.*** In a rough draft, you might identify patterns of sentence-level, or local, errors instead of marking individual errors. Identifying patterns—representative strengths and limitations—helps students gain control over their writing and saves you time because you don't need to comment on every instance of the problem.

Tips for responding to student writers, *continued*

- ***Anchor comments.*** Anchor your comments in a student's text to avoid vague directives. If a student has written, "Cultural differences make it difficult for Italian students to study in the United States," an anchored comment can give better direction. Instead of writing "Examples?!" try a comment like this: "You can strengthen your point by including two or three examples of the kinds of cultural differences you mean."
- ***Plant seeds.*** Responding is more effective when the language of comments grows from conversations and lessons in the classroom. Students shouldn't be encountering terms or ideas for the first time in the margins of their papers. If you write, "You've presented the evidence; now analyze the evidence," it's best if you've talked in class about what it means to analyze evidence.
- ***Teach one lesson at a time.*** Reading an entire draft, quickly, before commenting may actually save time. Ask: What single lesson (or two) do I want to teach here? And how will my comments teach this lesson? Heading into each draft with these questions will keep your comments consistent and focused and will help you develop a hierarchy of concerns appropriate for the draft, which may keep you from over-commenting. Keep in mind that there is a finite set of lessons an individual student can learn in revising a single paper.
- ***Direct students to handbook help.*** For surface-level errors, link comments to specific handbook lessons. You don't have to use your time to teach lessons about sentence fragments or subject-verb agreement if you assign a handbook. Use a shorthand system to point students to advice and examples in the handbook. If you and your students are all using *A Writer's Reference*, you can direct them to edit fragments by using the shorthand *frag* in the margin or a code like G5-c. Remember that if you notice a pattern of sentence boundary errors, point out the pattern, but don't edit every instance.

Encouraging revision

- ***Tread purposefully and lightly.*** Avoid leaving too heavy a footprint in the margins of students' papers. Use your comments to show students how to start revising without suggesting specific language for the revision.
- ***Begin the dialogue.*** Ask students to submit a rough draft along with a cover letter or "Dear Reader" letter. A "Dear Reader" letter reminds students that they are writing for a reader, allows them to begin a dialogue about their work, and provides an opportunity for them to articulate their specific questions and concerns. Always ask students to identify their favorite part of their paper in the "Dear Reader" letter.

Tips for responding to student writers, *continued*

- ***Make a plan.*** When you hand back drafts with your comments, assign students to review the comments, perhaps during the final fifteen minutes of a class, and to write a one-page revision plan in which they explain what they learned from the comments and how they plan to use the comments as they revise.

Responding to final drafts

- ***Refresh your memory.*** Before responding to final drafts, reread the assignment and the expectations you may have listed for students. Doing so keeps you grounded in a specific context and keeps the commentary tied to the assignment.
- ***Put final comments in context.*** On a final draft, evaluate the strengths and limitations in the context of the assignment's goals. For you, responding is far easier when the goals of an assignment are specific and when those goals have shaped the language and lessons that prepared students for the assignment.
- ***Provide a bridge.*** Writers develop their skills over time. It's too much to expect that first-year writing teachers can cover every lesson students need to write successfully across the curriculum. Make sure your comments on final drafts do double duty. Final comments can evaluate success in relation to the specific assignment, but they should also provide a bridge—or a transportable lesson—to the next assignment or to assignments in other courses.

Manufactured in the United States of America.

9 8 7 6 5 4

f e d c b a

For information, write: Bedford/St. Martin's, 75 Arlington Street, Boston, MA 02116 (617-399-4000)

ISBN 978-1-4576-9800-2